# STUPID GHOST
by Savannah Reich

Characters:

GHOST, female.

RONNIE, female.

JJ, male.

POLTERGEIST, no gender in particular.

LECTURER, any gender.

MAN IN CAR - played by JJ.
BARISTA - played by Ronnie.
DRIVER - played by JJ.


Note: The actor's genders do not necessarily need to match those of the characters they play.

*ALL RIGHTS RESERVED*
*Original Works Publishing*

CAUTION: Professionals and amateurs are hereby warned that this play is subject to royalty. It is fully protected by Original Works Publishing and the copyright laws of the United States. All rights, including professional, amateur, motion pictures, recitation, lecturing, public reading, radio broadcasting, television, and the rights of translation into foreign languages are strictly reserved.

The performance rights to this play are controlled by Original Works Publishing and royalty arrangements and licenses must be secured well in advance of presentation. No changes of any kind shall be made to the work, including without limitation any changes to characterization, intent, time, place, gender or race of the character. PLEASE NOTE that amateur royalty fees are set upon application in accordance with your producing circumstances. When applying for a royalty quotation and license please give us the number of performances intended, dates of production, your seating capacity and admission fee. Royalty of the required amount must be paid whether the play is presented for charity or gain and whether or not admission is charged. Royalties are payable with negotiation from Original Works Publishing.

Due authorship credit must be given anywhere the title appears, on all programs, printing and advertising for the play. The name of the Playwright must appear on a separate line, in which no other name appears, immediately beneath the title and in size and prominence of type equal to 50% of the largest, most prominent letter used for the title of the Work. No person, firm or entity may receive credit larger or more prominent than that accorded to the Playwright.

Copying from this book in whole or in part is strictly forbidden by law, and the right of performance is not transferable. The purchase of this publication does not constitute a license to perform the work.

Whenever the play is produced, the following notice must appear on all programs, printing, and advertising for the play on separate line:

**"Produced by special arrangement with**
**Original Works Publishing.**
**www.originalworksonline.com"**

*Cover photo by Louis Stein,*
*Courtesy of Carnegie Mellon University School of Drama.*

*Stupid Ghost*
© Savannah Reich
Trade Edition, 2025
ISBN 978-1-63092-147-7

*Also Available From
Original Works Publishing*

### **DARKER** by Catie O'Keefe

**Synopsis:** In search of a job, Max finds himself the new kid at the Industri-Light Bulb Factory. But his surroundings are all too familiar… and he's certain he has seen his boss somewhere before. Is he losing his mind, or is this the start of a very sick- and ultimately deadly- game? Max must uncover the truth, or accept a fate that will keep his life in a mind-numbing limbo.

**Cast Size:** 2 Males, 1 Female

*Stupid Ghost* was first presented at Carnegie Mellon University on April 23, 2015. The production was directed by Ben Gansky. The cast was as follows:

Ghost - Amanda Jerry
Poltergeist - Ryan Avalos
Lecturer - Stanley Weiner
Ronnie - Erika Olson
JJ - Adam Stern-Rand

## STUPID GHOST

*PART ONE.*

*(The sound of radio static.*

*Three ghosts in the woods. They wear bed sheets with holes cut out for the eyes.*

*The GHOSTS hold up umbrellas, clothes hangers and other pieces of trash into the air, searching for the sweet spot. Sometimes they make ghost noises, like "wooo wooo".*

*One GHOST throws off her bed sheet to reveal that she wears clothes caked in dirt, and a sign around her neck that says "GHOST".)*

GHOST: Boo! *(pause)* Just kidding. It's funny because I am a ghost. The joke is that a real ghost would never try to scare you, because ghosts would never want you to feel bad. You might be like, "What? I thought ghosts were sneaky and gross and they live in the bathroom mirror and try to reach out with their icicle fingers and steal your soul!" Wrong. It's not your fault but you're wrong.

*(The GHOSTS find the radio signal - the oldies station. They "woo" with pleasure.)*

GHOST: The real deal is that ghosts don't actually do anything. They just hang out in the woods and listen to the radio. It's pretty boring, and they're pretty bad at it, but they don't have anything else to do and it isn't bothering anyone. They don't want to get in the way. Ghosts are nice! Right guys? Guys!

OTHER GHOSTS: Woooo.

GHOST: They don't remember anything except for being in the woods. They don't care about anything or think about anything. They're just kind of there. This one ghost lived in the woods, and she definitely would have just stayed there forever, except for this one day something happened to her, and that something was that she saw this girl.

*(Enter RONNIE, wearing headphones and singing. She has a cardboard around her neck that says "PRETTY GIRL". The GHOSTS lose their radio signal and stare.)*

GHOST: And because she saw the girl some things ended up happening. But it's important to remember that everything that she did was just what anyone would have done, if anyone was a ghost who had been living in the woods, mostly in silence, maybe forever.

*(RONNIE sings.)*

*(The GHOSTS follow her. The GHOSTS sing along. This is perhaps a full musical number.)*

GHOST: Sometimes these ghosts followed someone for just a little ways, but it wasn't a big deal. The person wouldn't even notice. And they would stop really really quickly. Usually they would stop right here.

*(The GHOST stops. Another ghost, the POLTERGEIST, goes on following RONNIE.)*

GHOST: What are you doing?

*(POLTERGEIST stops. They throw off their bed sheet, revealing a sign that says "ALSO A GHOST". RONNIE walks offstage.)*

POLTERGEIST: Beg your pardon?

GHOST: Are you stopping?

POLTERGEIST: I thought I might go just a little further.

GHOST: Oh!

POLTERGEIST: Unless you think I shouldn't.

GHOST: No, I don't mind.

POLTERGEIST: She won't even notice.

GHOST: Right, absolutely.

POLTERGEIST: Unless... you were going to?

GHOST: Oh no!

POLTERGEIST: I don't want to step on your toes.

GHOST: I don't follow people. I mean, I'm sorry. I don't mean to criticize you.

POLTERGEIST: No, no!

GHOST: I just wouldn't do it personally. Because I wouldn't want to scare her or anything. But if you want to…

POLTERGEIST: No, you're right. I don't want to scare anyone.

GHOST: Yeah, you never know.

POLTERGEIST: Can't be too careful.

GHOST: That's what I always say.

POLTERGEIST: All right, have a nice evening!

GHOST: You too! Don't follow anyone! Ha ha!

POLTERGEIST: Ha ha! Right, you either!

*(POLTERGEIST exits. GHOST looks at the audience.)*

GHOST: Ghosts are nice!

*(GHOST looks around, quickly catches up with RONNIE and follows her through the woods.)*

GHOST: This ghost usually never followed people. And she definitely never followed anyone all the way home and into their bedroom. It was a one-time thing.

*(RONNIE walks into her bedroom and begins undressing. The GHOST follows her.)*

GHOST: Hi. Can you hear me? Okay, so let's pretend that we're in your bedroom and we're friends and you invited me to come over. And you had this weird day and I'm like, ohmigod, tell me all about your day! Can you hear me? You can't hear me. Can you hear me?

*(Pause.)*

GHOST: Omigod, tell me all about your day!

POLTERGEIST (off): Veronica!

RONNIE: I'll be out in a minute!

GHOST: Veronica. Hi, Veronica. Hi.

POLTERGEIST (off): Sweetheart, is there a lock on your door?

RONNIE: Hold on, I'll get it.

*(RONNIE unlocks the door. Enter the POLTERGEIST, in a housedress and wig. The sign around their neck now reads, "MOTHER (POSSESSED)".)*

POLTERGEIST: Now, darling, I hardly think that's necessary.

*(The POLTERGEIST waves at the GHOST while RONNIE isn't looking.)*

GHOST: What are you *doing*?

RONNIE: I'm sorry. I just thought a little privacy could be nice.

GHOST: Get out of here!

POLTERGEIST: Do you think that you need to lock the door against anyone in this house?

GHOST: That's not your mom!

RONNIE:  All the girls at school have them.

POLTERGEIST:  I don't find it very "hip" to keep your own mother locked out of your bedroom.

RONNIE:  I'm sorry.

GHOST:  Oh my *god*.

POLTERGEIST:  It is my own home, after all.

RONNIE:  I know. I'm sorry.

POLTERGEIST:  It's all right, darling. I just don't want you to get swept up in trying to impress the popular crowd.

GHOST:  What are you even *talking* about?

RONNIE:  I'm not sure why I had it at all.

POLTERGEIST:  I'll just hold on to it and we won't speak of it again. And I'd like you to stay home tonight.

RONNIE:  But I was going to meet up with JJ.

POLTERGEIST:  Not tonight, dear.

*(The POLTERGEIST kisses RONNIE's head.)*

GHOST: Don't touch her!

*(The POLTERGEIST winks at the GHOST and leaves the room. RONNIE shakes her head, gets a towel and exits to the bathroom.)*

GHOST: The girl didn't act like she noticed anything weird, which the ghost thought was crazy. But maybe she did notice and just didn't say. It was hard for the ghost to know what the girl was thinking because she was so pretty. It always looked like she was thinking about flowers or something.

*(In another part of the house, the POLTERGEIST is doing something odd with kitchen utensils and white flour.)*

GHOST: Um. Excuse me.

POLTERGEIST: Yes?

GHOST: Sorry if I was rude, before. I was just surprised to see you here.

POLTERGEIST: No problem.

GHOST: Since you said you were going back.

POLTERGEIST: Sure. I understand.

GHOST: Um. What are you doing?

POLTERGEIST: Oh, you know. Cooking dinner.

GHOST: Okay. But-

*(The GHOST indicates the POLTERGEIST's appearance.)*

POLTERGEIST: Oh, this? This is actually her mother. Cute, right?

GHOST:  You can't do that.

POLTERGEIST:  Oh please. I do it all the time.

GHOST:  Are you serious?

POLTERGEIST:  Don't be so dramatic. Do you want me to help you? It's really easy.

GHOST:  No. No thank you.

POLTERGEIST:  Okay. My mistake.

GHOST:  You said you didn't follow people.

POLTERGEIST:  So did you.

*(The POLTERGEIST "cooks" gleefully.)*

GHOST:  It's not the same thing!

POLTERGEIST:  Do you see any eggs?

GHOST:  Did you hear me? It's not the same thing!

POLTERGEIST:  Fine, that's fine. Why don't you go check on her, she's about to get out of the bath. Dinner's almost ready.

*(The GHOST turns to the audience.)*

GHOST:  It was not the same thing.

POLTERGEIST:  Of course!

*(The GHOST returns to the bedroom. RONNIE's arm shoots out from behind the bathroom door, groping for her bathrobe. The GHOST hands it to her. RONNIE enters, tying the sash of the robe, and sits at her vanity mirror. She makes faces in the mirror. The GHOST stands behind her, looking at their reflections in the mirror and copying RONNIE's every move.)*

GHOST: Don't worry about anything because I'm going to keep you safe. You know like when someone has a ghost but it's their friend? I'm going to stay right next to you and you'll be like "huh, why do I feel so safe" and you won't know it's because I'm with you all the time, every second, I'm right here with you.

JJ stands in the front yard. He wears a sign around his neck that says "TEENAGE BOY".

JJ: Hey! Ronnie!

GHOST: This was the first time the ghost ever saw JJ.

*(RONNIE opens her second-floor bedroom window. She and JJ have both looked forward to this moment all day.)*

RONNIE: Hi!

JJ: Hey! I guess everyone's going down to the lake tonight.

RONNIE: I can't go out.

JJ: Aw, for real?

RONNIE: My mom wants me to stay in. I have a lot of homework anyways.

JJ: Lame.

GHOST: At first the ghost did not really think he was that great.

RONNIE: Will you miss me?

JJ: Nope.

RONNIE: Stop it!

JJ: I'll just get a new girlfriend.

RONNIE: Shut up!

GHOST: Not even funny, in her opinion.

RONNIE: You don't have homework?

JJ: I dunno, not really. College stuff.

RONNIE: Your applications?

JJ: Yeah.

RONNIE: Did you decide which ones you're gonna do?

JJ: I don't know, kind of. Look, I don't really like to talk about this stuff with you.

RONNIE: Why not?

JJ: Because, you know. Because I'm leaving next year and you're not. And I feel weird talking to you about it, because I get to leave in like less than a year. And I'm gonna be in some cool city meeting all these new people and seeing all this cool stuff without you, and I just don't want to make you feel bad.

RONNIE: Oh.

*(Pause.)*

JJ: I feel like I said something wrong, but I don't know what it was.

RONNIE: No, it's fine. Have fun at the lake.

JJ: Wait, Ronnie, what's up? Are you mad?

RONNIE: I'm not mad.

JJ: Don't be mad.

RONNIE: I said I'm not mad.

JJ: Hey, I was thinking about you today when I was in ceramics.

RONNIE: Oh yeah?

JJ: Yeah, I was making this like, jar? Only it was coming out really really bad. And then I was like, how do I know it's bad? I've only ever seen like ten kinds of jars. I've only ever known like 100 people. How do I know what I think about anything? Like maybe everything I think I know is wrong.

*(The GHOST walks closer to JJ, examining him closely.)*

RONNIE: You said you were thinking about me?

JJ: Oh yeah. I don't remember now.

RONNIE: Oh.

JJ: Hey, I finished that song. If you still want to hear it.

**(For an alternate scene where JJ does not sing, see appendix. Each production may set the song to music however they choose.)**

RONNIE: Oh great!

JJ: Is that- should I just?

RONNIE: Sure. I have time for one song.

GHOST: Just one, though.

JJ: Okay. It's not like one hundred per cent done so, whatever, if you don't like it that's okay.

*(JJ plays guitar and sings. It is simple and sweet. Maybe the GHOST joins in.)*

SONG: "You Make It Look Easy"

   Getting out of bed
   Wearing pants that are
   The nice kind
   Walking down the road
   Waving hello at

The right time

You make it look easy

Smiling with your face
Sitting quiet with
Your feet still
Dancing with your mom
Asking waiters for a refill

You make it look easy
You make it look so easy

*(The song ends. JJ is suddenly embarrassed.)*

JJ: Yeah, so.

RONNIE: It's really good.

*(The GHOST stands very close to JJ. She sniffs him.)*

JJ: I'd actually prefer if you didn't say anything about whether you liked it or not. Just, like... I should probably just go.

RONNIE: I liked it!

JJ: Kay. You don't have to say that though.

RONNIE: It's really good.

JJ: Okay. Whatever. See you in class.

RONNIE: Bye.

JJ: Bye.

RONNIE: See you tomorrow!

GHOST: And the ghost was like: whoa.

*(RONNIE goes back into her bedroom and sits at the vanity. GHOST puts her hand to her ear like a telephone.)*

GHOST: Ring ring. Ring ring.

*(RONNIE answers her actual telephone.)*

RONNIE: Hello?

GHOST: Hi. Is "Ronnie" there?

RONNIE: This is she.

GHOST: Hi. It's me.

RONNIE: Who?

GHOST: You know.

RONNIE: Alison?

GHOST: Yeah.

RONNIE: Your voice sounds funny.

GHOST: Yeah. Um, I've got a cold.

RONNIE: Listen, my life is falling apart.

GHOST: Omigod, tell me all about it.

RONNIE: My mom is being so weird.

GHOST:  You're so pretty.

RONNIE:  What?

GHOST:  Like, your hair seems really clean, and the way your face looks and everything.

RONNIE:  Oh... thank you?

GHOST:  Your boyfriend is pretty too. I think you should get married.

RONNIE:  Alison!

GHOST:  And maybe don't talk to your mom ever again.

RONNIE:  What?

GHOST:  She's just jealous of you. Because, you know, not everyone can understand what it feels like to be a really special person like you are. And you're just so pretty, and you go to high school and live in a house, and some people are just going to get jealous.

RONNIE:  Do you have a fever or something?

GHOST:  No. Why?

RONNIE:  You sound kind of funny.

GHOST:  What do you mean?

RONNIE:  I don't know. I guess I'm just tired. I should go do my homework.

GHOST: But your life is falling apart!

RONNIE: You know, it's not really that big of a deal. I was just being dramatic. I should probably just do my homework and forget about it.

GHOST: Are you mad at me?

RONNIE: No, of course not! I'm gonna hang up the phone now though, okay? You should get some sleep.

GHOST: I'm not tired!

RONNIE: Okay, well, I've gotta go. I'll see you tomorrow, okay Alison?

GHOST: We're friends, right?

RONNIE: Yeah. We're friends.

GHOST: Can I call you later?

RONNIE: I have to go! Bye!

*(RONNIE hangs up the phone.)*

GHOST: I'm sorry. You think I'm weird. Oh god, I shouldn't have called. I should have just left you alone. Aren't you glad I'm here? Just a little bit? Can't you just kind of tell?

*(RONNIE walks out of the room, brushing right by the GHOST.)*

*(Crushed, the GHOST goes to look in the mirror again. She picks up a headband that RONNIE was wearing earlier and puts it on. She checks her reflection.)*

GHOST: This is the part where the ghost decided that she should probably just go home.

*(She starts to take the headband off, hesitates, then decides to keep it.*

*The GHOST walks out of the house and shivers in the cold. She steels herself to walk back into the woods.*

*JJ enters.)*

JJ: Whoa! Hey! Ronnie? Hello? Are you okay?

*(The GHOST looks behind her, then realizes with a start that he is talking to her.)*

GHOST: What?

JJ: I thought you had homework.

GHOST: Yeah.

JJ: Okay. Did you finish it?

GHOST: Um, no. I'm just, um.

JJ: Taking a walk?

GHOST: Yeah.

JJ: Um, okay. Well, do you want to hang out later, or...?

GHOST: Oh, no. I should... I should go.

JJ: Back home.

GHOST: Yes.

JJ: To do your homework.

GHOST: Yes.

JJ: Okay. Are you... sad?

*(A pause. She answers honestly.)*

GHOST: Yes.

JJ: Is it like, cause you can't go to the lake with everyone?

GHOST: Yes.

JJ: Well, let's go out to the lake tomorrow. Okay? We can use my dad's canoe.

GHOST: All right.

JJ: Okay. Well, I'll see you tomorrow.

*(He leans in to kiss her on the cheek. She flinches away.)*

JJ: High five?

*(He holds up his hand. Instead of slapping it, she touches it softly.)*

JJ: Oh. Um, okay. I'll see you.

GHOST: I'll see you too!

*(JJ exits. The GHOST looks at the audience, too dazed to know what to say.)*

POLTERGEIST: As it turns out, she did not go home.

GHOST: No.

POLTERGEIST: She walked downtown and stood under a streetlight. Every now and then someone would walk right past her, and some of them would even nod. Cars honked at her because they could see her.

*(The GHOST looks around, amazed.)*

MAN IN CAR: Hey baby, you need a ride somewhere?

POLTERGEIST: Silence.

MAN IN CAR: Hey, what's the matter with you?

POLTERGEIST: Silence.

MAN IN CAR: The hell with you.

POLTERGEIST: She went into a coffee shop and waited in line. When it was her turn, the woman looked right at her and spoke to her.

BARISTA: What can I get for you?

POLTERGEIST: Silence.

BARISTA: Hello? Can you hear me? You want a coffee or something? All right, come on, I've got customers waiting here. Let's go, get out of the way. Nope, you can't sit in here. Go on. Shoo.

POLTERGEIST: And after the shops all closed she just walked in the street, right in the middle of the road. Every now and then a car would come and she would just stand there, not moving. And the car would stop.

*(The GHOST stretches her arms out. The SCREECH of a car braking.)*

DRIVER: Get out of the road! What are you, crazy?

GHOST: It would stop for <u>her</u>.

*(BLACKOUT.)*

## PART TWO.

*(Lights up on the POLTERGEIST, lounging in the living room.*

*JJ enters. He doesn't see the POLTERGEIST.)*

POLTERGEIST: Hello JJ.

*(JJ jumps.)*

JJ: Oh! Oh my god. Sorry. I didn't see you there.

POLTERGEIST: Why don't you sit down, sweet pea? I've got a pie in the oven.

JJ: Oh, no thanks. I mean, I'm supposed to meet Ronnie, we were gonna go down to the lake tonight.

POLTERGEIST: Just while you wait. She's not home quite yet.

JJ: Oh. I thought I was supposed to meet her.

POLTERGEIST: You know, I've been thinking, JJ, that I'd like to ask you a few questions if you're going to continue, well I don't know what you kids call it nowadays. "Stepping out" with my daughter. Is that right?

JJ: Oh, no. I mean. Yes Ma'am.

POLTERGEIST: I don't think I'm quite old enough to be a "Ma'am", JJ. Give me a few more years.

JJ: Sorry.

POLTERGEIST: Now, your parents work down at the university, is that right?

JJ: Yeah. They're both professors, um, they actually met when my dad was a grad student at-

POLTERGEIST: So I guess they've already had a little talk with you about the birds and the bees.

JJ: Yes Ma'am. I mean, yeah.

POLTERGEIST: Was it your mother or your father?

JJ: My father.

POLTERGEIST: Of course it was. I'm sure he did a fine job, but there are some things that are really better left to us gals.

JJ: Okay.

POLTERGEIST: Now my Veronica is a sweetheart, and I try to help her all I can, but you know what they say, there's no substitute for the old university of life. Look at me for example. Now, you might not believe it, but some people tell me I'm still quite a dish. Don't you agree?

JJ: Yes. Absolutely.

POLTERGEIST: Now the secret of my success, as it were, is that I have always said that it's not the cards you've got, it's how you shuffle. We girls know that effort makes all the difference. In just the same way, when you are being "intimate" with my daughter, I think you'll find-

JJ: We're not- we haven't-

POLTERGEIST: Now just listen- I think you'll find that the sweet bloom of youth will only take you so far. At some point you'll start to wish there was someone who had been to a few more rodeos, so to speak. Someone who could give you a few tips.

JJ: You know, I think maybe I was supposed to meet Ronnie down at the dock, this must have been some kind of mix up.

POLTERGEIST: I just want you to know, JJ, that I'm here for you if you have any questions about anything at all. Anything at all.

JJ: Um, sure. Thanks a lot. I'm going to go down to the docks and wait, could you tell Ronnie I'm there? I mean, I think she must be there waiting for me, but just in case, um, I'll be there. Thank you.

POLTERGEIST: Enjoy yourself now!

JJ: Um. Thank you. Goodnight.

*(JJ escapes. The POLTERGEIST laughs.*

*Enter the GHOST. She is dressed in RONNIE's clothes.)*

POLTERGEIST: Well look at you.

GHOST: I didn't do it on purpose.

POLTERGEIST: I see.

GHOST: It just happened.

POLTERGEIST: Well that's handy!

GHOST: But I'm not- I mean, it's still different than what you do. Right?

POLTERGEIST: Sure!

GHOST: I'm not doing anything to her. She's still okay. Right?

POLTERGEIST: You know, this is just perfect. I know something that is going to make you very happy.

GHOST: What?

POLTERGEIST: Guess!

GHOST: No.

POLTERGEIST: Oh, fine, I'll just tell you. That young man is waiting for you down at the lake.

GHOST: Where is Ronnie?

POLTERGEIST: She's at school!

GHOST: It's too late for school.

POLTERGEIST: It's perfect. He won't even know the difference.

GHOST: He thinks I'm her.

POLTERGEIST: Yes, dear.

GHOST: I didn't do anything wrong.

POLTERGEIST: Of course you didn't!

GHOST: She should be home by now.

POLTERGEIST: No no no. She's perfectly fine. Go on and enjoy your little date. I heard he's taking you out in a canoe!

GHOST: Taking her out.

POLTERGEIST: What's the difference? Go on! Have a little fun! Shoo!

*(The GHOST leaves the room.)*

GHOST: The ghost walked down to the docks as the sun was setting. She considered that Ronnie could be a number of places.

POLTERGEIST: She could be at school, where she was very possibly engaged in some extracurricular activities.

GHOST: The ghost imagined that Ronnie was a part of the yearbook committee, and was probably out where kids were playing frisbee or having fun with their friends, and their friends were her friends too so it wasn't weird at all when she asked if she could take their picture.

POLTERGEIST: Say Cheese!

GHOST: The ghost definitely would have gone home if she thought that Ronnie wasn't absolutely fine.

POLTERGEIST: She was a very nice ghost.

RONNIE: Let me out!

*(RONNIE pounds against her bedroom door. The POLTERGEIST saunters over and leans on the other side.)*

POLTERGEIST: What's that, sweetheart?

RONNIE: I have to go to the bathroom!

POLTERGEIST: Number one or a number two?

RONNIE: Just let me out! Please!

POLTERGEIST: I'm sorry honey, but like I told you before, I can't do that right now.

RONNIE: I swear I didn't do anything!

POLTERGEIST: Well, I think we both know that's not true.

*(RONNIE turns and addresses the audience.)*

RONNIE: Ronnie was not on the yearbook committee, and she wouldn't be even if you paid her one million dollars. The ghost couldn't imagine where Ronnie was because she never bothered to learn even the tiniest bit about her, not even one teeny tiny thing.

GHOST: Don't.

RONNIE: No one knew anything about Ronnie, not the stupid ghost, not her stupid mother who was honestly always like this even before she was possessed by anything, especially when she was drinking, not that Ronnie ever talked about it, not that anyone knew, not even her stupid boyfriend who suddenly decided that he would stop picking up his stupid phone.

GHOST: I said quit it!

RONNIE: The ghost thought they had some special connection, but they never did, it was a goddamn fantasy.

POLTERGEIST: Veronica!

RONNIE: What?

POLTERGEIST: I'm not sure I like that tone of voice.

*(JJ enters with a canoe paddle. He sits down and waits. The GHOST is torn between going to him and returning to the house.)*

RONNIE: I'm not talking to you!

POLTERGEIST: Well, I can hear you, and your tone of voice affects the people around you.

RONNIE: I'm not trying to annoy you. I really just...

POLTERGEIST: What is it, dear?

RONNIE: Can I just come out there and talk to you? I think there's been some kind of misunderstanding.

POLTERGEIST: Okay, how about this. Let's pretend that I'm your mother and you lied to me. So now I'm going to keep you in your room to teach you a lesson.

RONNIE: You are my mother!

POLTERGEIST: No, I know, but just for fun!

RONNIE: I don't know what you're talking about!

POLTERGEIST: Now, Veronica, this is the second time that I've had to mention your tone.

GHOST: There was some part of her that knew that Ronnie wasn't in an extracurricular activity, and she knew it and she knew she knew it but it was just one night, okay? I mean, it's not like she didn't get it. She understood. She knew it probably wasn't going to be the most magical perfect night ever. And even if it was, he probably wasn't going to look into her eyes and fall in love with her. Obviously.

*(Pause.)*

GHOST: She just thought... whatever. One night. One night is not that big of a big deal.

*(JJ and the GHOST get into the canoe. JJ paddles. The GHOST sits backward in the front and stares at him intensely.*

*Silence. JJ slaps a mosquito.)*

JJ: Buggy out.

GHOST: Do you have a favorite thing?

JJ: What?

GHOST: Color?

JJ: No. I mean... no.

GHOST: JJ. Look at me.

JJ: What?

GHOST: That's all.

JJ: Okay. I'm gonna look away now.

GHOST: Okay.

*(She points to something in the water.)*

GHOST: What is that?

JJ: Um, I think that's a beer can. Yup.

GHOST: Wow.

JJ: Are you... did something happen today?

GHOST: Why?

JJ: You're being kind of intense.

GHOST: I'm having several emotions.

JJ: Okay. That's cool. I still don't know what I'm going to be for Halloween.

GHOST: What you're going to "be"?

JJ: Yeah, cause I thought I could be like, just a zombie? But I feel like everyone always does that. I have this like weird vest that used to be my mom's that has a bunch of cats on it, but I'm not sure what that would be a costume for.

GHOST: I don't care about that.

JJ: Oh. Okay.

GHOST: I only want to say things that are really important.

JJ: I don't know if I'm very good at that.

GHOST: Just pretend we only have one amount of time.

JJ: What?

GHOST: Like one amount of time left and then that's it.

JJ: What amount of time?

GHOST: One night.

JJ: Like a last night on earth?

GHOST: Kind of.

JJ: I think about that all the time.

GHOST: Serious?

JJ: Yeah sure. I mean, that's the thing. What would you do? Would you run around stealing cars and stuff? It's like that's what you're supposed to say but I don't think I actually would. And I would feel like I should say goodbye to people but then what's the point, if you have to say goodbye to everyone? You know?

GHOST: I would be with you.

JJ: I feel like I would want to be alone.

GHOST: Why would you want that?

JJ: I don't know. Seems like it would be too sad to be with anyone else.

GHOST: You would have the rest of your life to be alone.

JJ: But there is no rest of your life. That's the whole point.

GHOST: What is that?

JJ: Bats. I think those are bats. They fly around, like, erratically like that, because they're chasing bugs. I mean I think I heard that.

GHOST: Oh my god. BATS BATS BATS!

JJ: Whoa, hey.

GHOST: It's okay. They like it.

JJ: God. I want to be feeling what you're feeling right now.

GHOST: You should be.

JJ: It seems like you are really into this right now.

GHOST: I am so into this right now.

JJ: Sometimes I worry that I have a problem with that stuff.

GHOST: What stuff?

JJ: I guess, feeling things?

GHOST: Oh no!

JJ: No, it's okay. It's not a big deal.

GHOST: Yes it is!

JJ: No no, it's fine. I think it's not what you're thinking. It's not like... I mean, I'm not miserable or anything. But people in books and movies are always like, "I'm so passionate about this thing, and I'm gonna go battle these gremlins or whatever, and I don't even care if I die, because I know I believe in... you know. Whatever." I don't know. Maybe that's an unrealistic expectation.

GHOST: No.

JJ: I don't know why I'm talking about this.

GHOST: You have to talk about it.

JJ: No, I'm making it sound like it's a big deal. It's really not. I just feel, I guess, like I can't really just experience things any more, I have to be thinking about them or watching them or just, you know, <u>knowing</u> all along that there's something so embarrassing about everything I'm doing. And if the future me could see me, he would say you're so stupid. You're being so stupid.

GHOST: Do you feel like that right now?

JJ: Oh, yeah. Completely.

*(The GHOST invents a thing called a kiss. It is sort of, but not exactly, like a human kiss. It is weird, but also hot.)*

JJ: Whoa!

GHOST: What?

JJ: You seem different.

*(Another "kiss". The GHOST whispers in JJ's ear. He seems shocked.)*

JJ: You mean...

GHOST: Yes.

JJ: I thought you had this whole thing about it being special.

GHOST: Whatever.

JJ: You seem weird tonight, okay? Are you like, on some kind of, I don't know, medication?

GHOST: I am sitting right in front of you.

JJ: Okay. What?

GHOST: I am saying I want to. I am saying that.

JJ: Right.

GHOST: This is special. This is very special to me.

JJ: Yeah, okay, but we didn't like... I mean I feel like we should talk about it some more.

GHOST: I don't know how anything will ever be more special than this time right now. Right this second. You're here, and I'm here, and there's bats, and what is not special about this?

JJ: I don't know.

GHOST: This is special. This is what special feels like, is this.

JJ: Okay.

GHOST: Okay?

JJ: Okay.

*(She begins to take off her clothes.)*

JJ: Whoa! Not in the boat.

GHOST: Why not?

JJ: Well, it's dark. And we don't have any running lights or anything. I didn't bring a lifejacket.

GHOST: A "life jacket"?

JJ: It's just basic water safety. Let's go to the island.

*(They abandon the boat and run offstage.*

*The POLTERGEIST returns to RONNIE's bedroom door.)*

POLTERGEIST: Veronica. I don't think it's unreasonable of me to expect an apology.

RONNIE *(Patiently)*: For what?

POLTERGEIST: You don't need to scream at me, I'm right here.

RONNIE: I didn't!

POLTERGEIST: You were always such a sweet little girl. It's sad.

RONNIE: I would be happy to apologize if you would tell me what you think I did.

POLTERGEIST: You think I enjoy keeping you in there? This hurts me.

RONNIE: Okay, can you just-

POLTERGEIST: I really don't think it's fair of you to do this, you know I don't like to punish you. I feel absolutely awful.

RONNIE: I don't understand what you want from me.

POLTERGEIST: Are you sure?

RONNIE: Can you tell me? Please?

POLTERGEIST: I think if you really think about it, you already know.

RONNIE: I really, really don't.

POLTERGEIST: Well. It's just what we all want. It's what all of us want from all of you.

RONNIE: Who is "us"?

POLTERGEIST: All of us... you know. All of us "moms". It's just what all moms want from their children.

RONNIE: Okay. What is that?

POLTERGEIST: We're not there yet, honey. Let's start with a simple apology.

RONNIE: Okay, fine. I'm sorry.

POLTERGEIST: A little conviction, please.

RONNIE: I'm so, so sorry, I didn't mean to do it, and I wish I hadn't, and I will do whatever it takes to never, never do it again.

POLTERGEIST: Do what again?

RONNIE: I don't...

POLTERGEIST: Use your words, Veronica.

RONNIE: Why are you doing this?

POLTERGEIST: I'm not doing this, Veronica. You're doing this. I don't know what happened, but you've changed.

RONNIE: I did?

POLTERGEIST: You think I can't hear you? Getting up in the middle of the night, slicing up my good curtains, stealing all the popsicles from the freezer, I was saving those!

RONNIE: What popsicles!?!

*(POLTERGEIST slams their fist against the door, hard.)*

POLTERGEIST: Lying to my face! You're doing this to me, Veronica. You're making me keep you here. You're doing this.

RONNIE: I don't understand what you're talking about!

POLTERGEIST: Don't laugh at me! You think this is funny?

*(RONNIE is shocked- she was not laughing.)*

RONNIE: I wasn't!

*(The POLTERGEIST opens the door and pokes their head inside. RONNIE stares, frozen.*

*They begin slamming their head against the door as hard as they can, over and over. RONNIE screams.)*

POLTERGEIST: Veronica! Stop it! Stop it! Don't do this to me! Stop it!

*(They spit out a handful of teeth, which clatter across the floor.*

*RONNIE runs toward them, pushes the door open and escapes, knocking them onto the ground.*

*POLTERGEIST sits up, breathing heavily, and spits a little blood onto the floor. They laugh.)*

POLTERGEIST: Have a nice time, dear! Don't stay out too late!

*(JJ and the GHOST walk onto the island together. It is the greatest thing she has ever seen in her life. JJ sets down a boom box and presses play.*

*The GHOST stands with her eyes closed, listening to the music. She begins to twitch. She dances, waving her arms and legs around randomly.*

*JJ joins in, hesitantly at first, then letting himself get as wild as she is. They flail around like toddlers on the dance floor at a wedding. They dance for some time- maybe this is a full dance number.*

*They laugh at each other, then suddenly turn serious. They move together. They "kiss".*

*RONNIE stands on the shore yelling.)*

JJ: Do you hear something?

GHOST: No.

JJ: Do you mind if I turn this up?

*(He turns up the radio. The music blasts. Blackout.)*

## *PART THREE*

*(RONNIE stumbles onstage, looking rumpled and dirty. She dials a cell phone and walks in a circle as she talks. The GHOST enters, wearing an identical outfit.*

*She follows RONNIE at a safe distance, listening to her phone conversations. RONNIE never turns around.*

*JJ walks across the stage mechanically, without seeing either of them.)*

JJ: Yo, this is JJ, leave me a message if you want to, but I probably won't listen to it. Sorry. BEEP.

RONNIE: Hey it's me. I'm at the coffee shop downtown, but I think they might make me leave soon because I've been here a long time and I haven't bought anything. I don't know where I'm going to go, but I'll try to call you again soon, so... please please please call me back.

*(The GHOST addresses the audience. Her tone is soft and dreamy, as RONNIE begins to panic.)*

GHOST: In the morning, the ghost walked through the town and considered her options. She should probably go straight back to the woods. Also, the way the sunlight was hitting the store windows was amazing. Also there was one store that smelled like bread and one that smelled like gasoline. Also, she saw a dog!

*(The GHOST waves at the dog, thrilled.)*

RONNIE: Hey, it's me again. I guess you have your phone off, so I'm going to stop calling you, but I just... I'm really scared and I don't know where you are, and I don't really understand why you're not answering and I don't really understand anything.

GHOST: But she wasn't supposed to be there, smelling gasoline and seeing dogs. She was supposed to go home.

RONNIE: Hi, it's me. My phone is about to die, so, if you do want to see me, can you meet me at Christine's costume party later? Maybe you remember, we were supposed to go together? Or just call me, please, please call me.

*(A rotary dial telephone on wheels slides onto the stage and comes to rest near RONNIE's feet.*
*The GHOST holds up her hand like a telephone.)*

GHOST: Ring ring!

*(RONNIE looks down at the telephone on the ground.)*

RONNIE: Um, excuse me? Is anyone expecting a call?

GHOST: Ring ring!

RONNIE: Hello?

GHOST: Ronnie, it's Alison. Are you okay?

RONNIE: Who is this?

GHOST: I said it's Alison.

RONNIE: Who is this?

GHOST: I just want to make sure that you're alright.

RONNIE: I don't know how to answer that.

GHOST: Did something happen to you?

*(RONNIE laughs.)*

RONNIE: I don't know.

GHOST: Are you okay? Just tell me yes or no.

*(RONNIE laughs more, sounding increasingly unhinged.)*

GHOST: So you're basically all right.

*(RONNIE hangs up the phone and rolls it violently offstage.)*

GHOST: Ronnie? Hello?

*(JJ walks across the stage vacantly again.)*

JJ: Yo, this is JP, leave me a message if you want to, but I probably won't listen to it. Sorry. BEEP.

RONNIE: Just in case you're interested, I slept in a ditch last night.

GHOST:  JJ wasn't picking up his phone because it was out of batteries, because he slept on the island with a ghost. Also, ghosts sleep in a ditch every night.

RONNIE:  I swear to God, JJ, I spent so much time trying not to call you too many times. So you didn't think I was clingy. Because god forbid you should ever think for a second that I was clingy. But now I've called you like a hundred times and now that it's not easy anymore, you're gone. So why did I ever care so much what you think?

GHOST:  Some people don't ever get to wonder if they are being too clingy.

RONNIE *(laughing)*:  This feels crazy, but did I see you out on the lake last night with some girl? Like am I making that up? But it was you, I swear to god it was you. And now you just disappear? Like are you actually just going to never speak to me again?

GHOST:  The girl would probably spend the rest of her life going to parties, and talking on the telephone, and seeing dogs on the street.

RONNIE:  You know, I'm curious- what did you even like about me? What did you even know about me? You just thought I was *pretty* and *nice* and *fun*. And I wanted you to think I was *pretty* and *nice* and *fun*. I wanted everyone to think I was *pretty* and *nice* and *fun*. It's fun to be pretty and nice! It's nice to be fun and pretty! Except when all of a sudden your boyfriend disappears and you realize that he literally knows nothing about you! And he could just switch you out for some random girl at any moment! He looks at you and sees *nothing!*

*(Her laughter has slowly turned into rage).*

RONNIE: I guess you can't call me back! My phone is dead! See you at the party tonight or maybe never again, I really don't care anymore, bye!

GHOST: The ghost was very sorry. But she was going to that party.

*(The GHOST exits.*

*The ghost of a LECTURER comes onstage and addresses the audience. We have never seen this person before.)*

LECTURER: A Brief Taxonomy of Ghosts.

*(The LECTURER gestures to RONNIE that she should leave. RONNIE exits, confused.)*

LECTURER: Pardon me. If we could just take a moment of your time. It has come to our attention that we have neglected to define our terms. Our sincere apologies.

*(Maybe the LECTURER has a slideshow, or a large amount of papers, or hundreds of tiny scraps of paper that they throw in the air as they speak.)*

LECTURER: Specifically, we have neglected to specify the idea of "Ghost". A ghost, in this case, is not a loose and sentimental series of associations, but a kind of Genus, which is further divided into categories or species. We apologize for beginning this conversation so late in the game. We will attempt to be succinct.

The first and best-known category is ghosts of actual people who used to be alive.

Sub-category one: Special ghosts. If you have a special relationship with one or more of these ghosts, you may have brought them into this room with you. They are in the audience, not to watch the play, but to watch you as you watch it. This type of ghost is already well documented.

Sub-category two: Random ghosts. They are not attached to any specific person, but they might like to be. They are emotional, constantly embarrassed, easily confused. Again, well-documented. Most of the ghosts we've met tonight fall into this category.

Most people assume that all possible ghost knowledge ends here, but there are many, many other kinds of ghosts, more than we have time to mention today. Very briefly, some of the other categories include:

- Ghosts of people you thought you would become.
- Ghosts of ideas that were perfect in the abstract.
- Ghosts of passionate love for people who are currently inaccessible.
- Ghosts of children who are now adults.
- Ghosts of just-submerged mental imbalances.

- Ghosts of things you wanted to say but couldn't.
- Ghosts of yourself if you had been able to change.
- Ghosts of animals that you have disappointed.
- Ghosts of better-loved siblings.
- Ghosts of your own death, only occasionally and imperfectly understood.
- Ghosts of vacations on which you still weren't able to relax.
- Ghosts of the amount of time and effort that you thought something like this should take.
- Ghosts of movie stars to whom you bear a slight resemblance.
- Ghosts of favorite holiday decorations.
- Ghosts of the fun everyone had together before you got here.
- Ghosts of pure ecstasy, never to be attained again.
- Ghosts of past failure.
- Ghosts of the story you thought you were living.
- Ghosts of the unknowable abyss.

And so on. This list is by no means comprehensive but you begin to get the idea.

If each one of us is surrounded by a cloud of ghosts, then this audience is, mathematically speaking, more ghosts than people.

With this in mind, we would like to extend a special welcome to the ghosts here tonight. We would like to invite you to watch the show, if you'd like. If not, please enjoy the temperature, smells and noises in this room. We are pleased to share them with you.

Thank you for your patience. We will now return to the story.

*(The Lecturer exits. The GHOST enters, holding her bedsheet.)*

GHOST: Everyone at the party was wearing the same costume.

*(She puts on her bedsheet.*

*RONNIE, JJ and the POLTERGEIST, all dressed as ghosts in white bed sheets, come in to the party. They do not recognize each other.*

*Music begins. They dance. A choreographed group number. It is silly and full of joy; despite everything, this is a great party.*

*RONNIE stops and pulls her sheet off. She stares at two particular GHOSTS who are dancing together.*

*She pulls the sheet off one. It is JJ.*

*She pulls the sheet off the other. It is the GHOST.*

*JJ looks back and forth between RONNIE and the GHOST. His mind is unable to process what he is seeing.*

*RONNIE screams. The GHOST screams. JJ screams. RONNIE runs out of the party.)*

GHOST: Wait!

*(Everyone else runs after RONNIE.*

*The GHOST and JJ jump in a car and begin to careen across the stage. The GHOST drives, JJ sits shotgun.)*

GHOST: A car chase through the woods. Very dark. Gravel roads.

JJ: What the fuck- I can't, I can't-

GHOST: I really need you to stay calm-

JJ: Can you just explain to me-

GHOST: I need to concentrate-

JJ: Can you just explain to me what the fuck just happened-

GHOST: Don't yell at me don't yell at me DON'T YELL AT ME-

*(The POLTERGEIST rides through on a bicycle.)*

POLTERGEIST: Veronica! Where are you, Sugar?

*(RONNIE stumble-runs through the woods.)*

JJ: Ronnie I'm serious, slow down-

GHOST: Don't CALL me that-

JJ: I knew something was weird, I should have-

GHOST: Just shut up okay I don't have time for this-

JJ: You have to explain this to me, I can't just-

GHOST: It's my fault and I have to fix it-

JJ: What is your fault-

GHOST: It's your fault too-

JJ: Jesus- slow down!

*(RONNIE trips and gets back up, limping now.)*

POLTERGEIST: Veronica! Don't do anything silly before I get there!

JJ: Stop the car please just stop the car I want to get out-

GHOST: I need you to be looking for her just be quiet and look for her-

JJ: Ronnie I said stop the car-

GHOST: I said don't call me that-

POLTERGEIST: Wait for me, sweetheart!

JJ: Ronnie you're really freaking me out right now-

GHOST: I said stop it okay!

JJ: Stop what?

GHOST: This is not working anymore-

POLTERGEIST: I'm coming, my angel!

GHOST: What was that?

JJ: What-

GHOST: Did you see something-

*(The GHOST whips the car around.)*

POLTERGEIST: VERONICA!

JJ: Jesus I just want to go home please let me out Ronnie please stop the car I want to get out-

GHOST: You better stop calling me that-

JJ: Stop the car Ronnie-

GHOST: What are you stupid, you're so stupid-

JJ: Stop the car-

GHOST: Look at me, you idiot, look at my face!

*(JJ looks at her face and suddenly understands.)*

JJ: Oh my god-

POLTERGEIST: There she is!

*(RONNIE jumps out from the woods, arms outstretched. The POLTERGEIST shoots out in front of the car. The car swerves, brakes, fishtails.*

*Everyone speaks together as the car crashes in slow motion.)*

JJ *(Simultaneous)*: Oh shit I should have known I should have known something like this would happen I should have known better and now we're all gonna die I feel like my life is supposed to be flashing before my eyes shouldn't my life be flashing before my eyes? I guess I remember some stuff I remember puking in the kiddie pool in third grade and everyone screamed and got out, is that it, was that my life flashing? I thought it would be better than that I don't want this to be my last thought what's a good last thought what's the kind of thing you should be thinking about when you're in a car crash and you're about to die oh my god I don't want to die for this it's seriously too stupid to die right now I don't even know anything and it's too late now oh my god oh my god oh my god

GHOST *(Simultaneous)*: I'm sorry I'm sorry I'm sorry I'm sorry I'm sorry I'm sorry I'm sorry I'm sorry I'm sorry I'm sorry I'm sorry I'm sorry

RONNIE *(Simultaneous):* I want my funeral to be outside, and I don't want anyone to wear black. I want you to dress just casual like for a picnic. It'll be open casket and I'll be surrounded by flowers and my eyes will be open. You can walk by one by one and look into my eyes. You can tell each other that you wish you knew me better, you never realized how much you cared. But it's too late for that now. And you'll be sorry then, when you see me lying there surrounded by flowers, you'll be sorry then, you bunch of goddamn lying little shits, you'll be sorry then, motherfuckers, you'll be sorry then.

POLTERGEIST *(beginning at "motherfuckers")*: Woooooooo! Yeah! Woooooooooo!

*(A very loud CRASH.*

*Blackout.*

*RONNIE, JJ and the POLTERGEIST search for the radio signal, in the same formation as in the beginning. They do not wear bedsheets.*

*The GHOST speaks to the audience.)*

GHOST: I hope that this has been some helpful information for you regarding ghosts. They are not something that you need to worry about, because they would never, never hurt you.

*(RONNIE turns to glare at the GHOST.)*

GHOST: They would never hurt you on purpose.

*(RONNIE turns away.)*

GHOST: The point is that, um... in the end of the day...

*(The POLTERGEIST winks at her. The GHOST trails off.*

*RONNIE, JJ and the POLTERGEIST find the radio signal.*

*The GHOST smiles and begins to dance, wildly, the way she did on the island. She laughs out loud with joy as the other three ghosts stare blankly out into the darkness.)*

*END OF PLAY*

## *APPENDIX*

JJ: Don't be mad.

RONNIE: I said I'm not mad.

JJ: Hey, I was thinking about you today when I was in ceramics.

RONNIE: Oh yeah?

JJ: Yeah, I was making this like, jar? Only it was coming out really really bad. And then I was like, how do I know it's bad? I've only ever seen like ten kinds of jars. I've only ever known like 100 people. How do I know what I think about anything? Like maybe everything I think I know is wrong.

*(The GHOST walks closer to JJ, examining him closely.)*

RONNIE: You said you were thinking about me?

JJ: Oh yeah. I don't remember now.

RONNIE: Oh.

JJ: Sorry. Sorry. I feel like I want to be really nice to you all the time, because you're like, so pretty and smart and cool or whatever. But then I'm talking and it's just like, augh, what did I just say! Like what am I even talking about. Do you know what I mean? Probably not.

RONNIE: I know what you mean.

JJ:  Honestly, like in my mind I'm always thinking about all this nice stuff I want to do for you. Like I want you to wake up in the morning and look out your window, and there's like a million daffodils or something. Is that from a movie? I think that's from something. But there's like a million daffodils and I'm there, like singing a song about how you're like so pretty and cool. But then I'm like, where am I going to get all those daffodils, you know? Like do they sell them at like, a store? What store? And isn't that expensive, and bad for the environment probably? And I can't really sing. And maybe you would hate it anyways, cause it sounds really cheesy and awkward actually, like what are you supposed to do while I'm standing in the daffodils singing to you? Just like stand there? That sounds super weird. And then I'm like, maybe I don't know how to be nice to people and I just sort of make everything awkward and weird and I should just like, go away and disappear. You know?

*(The GHOST stands very close to JJ. She sniffs him.)*

RONNIE:  What is a daffodil?

JJ:  Well, I don't know. That's not really the point.

RONNIE:  Okay.

JJ:  It's more like, I'm an idiot.

RONNIE:  I don't think you're an idiot.

JJ: Okay. Well. Whatever. I don't know where to get daffodils, so I'm not going to bring you any.

RONNIE: That's fine.

JJ: I guess. Sorry I- I don't know. Sorry. I should go.

RONNIE: Okay. I don't think you're an idiot.

JJ: Okay. Well, see you in class.

*(JJ abruptly walks off.)*

RONNIE: See you tomorrow!

GHOST: And the ghost was like: whoa.

## NOTES

# NOTES

www.ingramcontent.com/pod-product-compliance
Lightning Source LLC
Chambersburg PA
CBHW061250040426
42444CB00010B/2326